Atmospheric Rivers

Brie Thomson

Atmospheric Rivers © 2022 Brie Thomson

All rights reserved.

No part of this publication may be reproduced, stored in a retrieval system, or transmitted, in any form or by any means, electronic, mechanical, photocopying, recording or otherwise, without the prior written permission of the presenters.

Brie Thomson asserts the moral right to be identified as author of this work.

Presentation by *BookLeaf Publishing*

Web: www.bookleafpub.com

E-mail: info@bookleafpub.com

ISBN: 978-93-95784-66-5

First edition 2022

ACKNOWLEDGEMENT

I would first like to thank and acknowledge the Sylix, Haudenosaunee, Chippewa, Mississauga, Anishinabeg and Wendat Nations, as these are the territories I unearthed the poems of this book on.

For everyone out there thinking they can't make it, thinking they don't belong in this world, that there's no one in their corner who understands what they're going through, I see you: keep fighting, I promise it's worth it.

Canning Days

I keep old jam jars because I am fascinated
by the way their curves and divets can hold
a scent, like fingers gripping canning tongs
tight, carefully lowering glass into water
the glass smells like home on those dreary
canning days
The scent of desert storms rolling down the
valley and summer-picked blackberries and
just enough sugar
The hum of bodies a well-known melody
here betwixt cabinets and countertops, it is
almost hymnal in nature
Conversations bubble like the mashed fruit
atop the stove, never moving above a
simmer
Instructions are spoken through movement
rather than words, we all think better by
doing
My mother has done this so often the recipe
has wound its memory into her muscles
I am still learning
still clumsy

Untitled

I will not take this for granted, I tell myself.
this, first time when the word family makes
sense
I can see us for our mosaic, all broken vase
glued back together to resemble our best
guess at love.
our best guess at family.
we are still growing, just as the earth is
always spinning
we are not Polaroids, snapshots that have not
felt air in their lungs since the darkness was
shook away,
we are flesh and life and blood, when cut we
still bleed
each day we come closer to fixing ourselves,
and that day will be magnificent

Kintsugi

3

I am picking up my own pieces
but my hands won't stop shaking
so I use the blood from my clumsy fingers
as glue and paint it red instead of gold

The Singular They

you say you cannot comprehend the singular
they
fine, then think of me as plural
my being is too complex to be defined as
singular anyway
They, referring to the myriad reincarnations
of this soul, the stops this train has made
before reaching mine
They, referring to all the people I have been,
all the people I will be, all the lives they
have led
They, being everyone I have met who has
influenced me
They, the ones who came before and paved
this way for me
Masculine or feminine are no matter, they
are both divine
you say you do not understand the singular
they, but I think what you really mean is that
growth makes you uncomfortable
you cannot fathom a life outside of your
small minded box and thus you think only in
squares

but I am infinite, an unending spiral twisting
figure eights betwixt your boxes into ever
expanding planes(*)
you may try to box me in, but you will not
hold me for long,
your cardboard reasoning is no match for
my switchblade tongue; you raised this
tongue, it got its sharpness from you
so I will put this into simpler terms for you:
I do not wish to be a boy, no, but in the same
fashion I do not wish to be a girl
I desire existence somewhere in between,
and they just feels like me

Untitled

under the desert sky
I sit and gaze at the morphology of the
clouds
ever-changing, in a state of constant flux
I wonder how they do it so effortlessly
if they too are scared to fall apart before
they reform
when the rains come, I soak myself to the
bone, hoping that by osmosis I can learn
their secrets, but I only ever end up with wet
socks and a runny nose
I have begun to wonder if the water particles
that make up clouds can feel pain
If they can, does it feel like this?

Sea Legs

maybe I just wanted a safe place to sleep
your arms happened to be a lighthouse in the
stormy seas of my endless nights
amber eyes like lanterns bobbing in the sea,
luring me to shore
under you my sea legs crumbled away like
sand in the sun and when you threw me back
in the water so abruptly I nearly drowned
I don't blame you, though, sirens are
supposed to be able to swim

Untitled

8

the history of my family is fraught, I cannot
find my roots
somewhere along the way I was grafted onto
this new tree and our rings don't line up
theirs are narrower, as if peeking through
blinds and I have never been good at
coloring inside the lines
I have yet to feel the weightlessness of
myself but I know I will someday unearth
her
if it takes until I am digging my own grave,
so mote it be, but I know, one day, I will find
me

Untitled

the fat phobia is deep rooted
It has wrapped its way up and around my
spine, holding me hostage like the puppet of
a tapeworm everyone wishes I would have
swallowed
every suggestion I hear is to lose a little
weight, but can't they see that I have tried
that? and that the pit of starvation in my
stomach brings me no comfort anymore?
when exclaiming that my old overalls were
now too small for me, my mother's
immediate suggestion was "maybe you
should lose a little weight?"
but why would I do that when I can just buy
new overalls?
I have been trapped under the weight of my
family's expectations for too long, as if this
fat body were baggage to be dragged and
resented
but where they see in themselves a couch
always being lugged up the stairs, as if their
bodies are the boulder and they are Sisyphus

I see the softest pillow known to man in the
curves of my thighs
I see a body that is marked by tenderness
I see arms meant for holding, and eyes
meant to be gazed into
I see constellations in my freckles as if the
night sky were inverted onto me
I feel the joy bubble in my laughter,
and I feel the universe flow through me
when I create, and not a single one of those
has a goddamned thing to do with how much
I weigh

Rewilding

I look at our made-up world going by like a
collage outside of the windows
our fabricated structures magazine cut-outs
against the hills
if only we could peel them back so easily:
the only residue reminding the earth of our
presence a little glue,
the torn edges of our papered towns
instead of our legacy of violence and
destruction and greed
returning the earth to itself may take more
lifetimes than we can imagine, the damage
we have done is so gross
my only prayer is that it is not too late to
turn the tides
that we can learn to live as one with the
earth again
before it is too late

Untitled

we were always doomed to fail
the earth is a Venus fly trap and we are the
parasite who thinks they have outsmarted
her
she has swallowed so many more whole
before us; we are still unearthing the bones
from her stomach
we thought she was sanctuary, but she has
always been digesting us
just think of what she will turn our remains
into, once her jaw finally snaps shut
it is her home, we are just living in it
and ungrateful houseguests we are, trashing
everything in sight and replacing her liquor
with poison
But while we weren't looking, she locked all
the doors
and as the music and lights cut out, you
realize the humidity you thought was just
bodies has always been her, and the pain in
your feet is from digestive acid
you never suspected her, and she used that to
her advantage.

Untitled

the late afternoon sun caresses the hills as if
they are old lovers
the clouds and their shadows, they cling, as
temporary things tend to do
but there is no hurry in the sun's gentle gaze
tendrils of light grasp the earth wherever
they meet, as if to say, hello my love, I
missed you, did you sleep well?
as they slip beneath the horizon, you can
hear them whisper, goodnight my love, I
will see you tomorrow.

Spinning Monkeys

It is a well-known fact that when you are
driving in a vehicle, if you come to a sudden
stop, your body will keep moving at the
same speed you were traveling.
I think that the same can be said in our daily
lives.
have you ever felt the aftershocks of
motion?
on the way home from the fair as a child
sitting in the car, and later at home, my body
would still be spinning monkeys well into
the night
after doing so all day, the abrupt unraveling
of my twisted bones felt wrong, like
straightening a spring.
my body, yearning for the motion to restart,
to dispel the conformity that has pulled my
muscles back into rigidness, attempts to
recreate the vertigo

Untitled

femininity has always felt like a distress
signal, but that may just be the hysterics
talking
I have been taught my entire life that being
"female" is two small steps from crazy, or
dead, it's as if being forced to constantly
walk a tightrope and then be told you're not
doing it right by someone who has never had
to worry about their footing
We are forced into bras like straightjackets
and told it's for our own good, and the men
still wonder why we are fearful, when our
pleas for equality were met with the
violence of your patronizing smile,
You treat us like wounded animals but you
are never ready for the consequences, don't
you know a wounded animal is more likely
to bite?

Untitled

Was I born to be an open wound? a bleeding
heart always making a mess on the floor?
or was I born to feel the pain those before
me repressed? flesh and bone turned time
capsule, but instead of pulling out records
and mementos, I am merely unrolling a thick
ball of crimson yarn
each kink a lesson formerly unlearned
but history cannot simply repeat endlessly
I am action and consequence, doomed to
weep, to hemorrhage until there is nothing
left and I crumble to dust in the wind
and if I am to bleed, who is it all for? is this
merely the final sonnet of my bloodline? my
life an audition to ensure my death throws
match the artistic visions of some higher
power?
Will I ever be more than nothing?

Untitled

I project my insecurities onto flowers
insist they must be perfect to be beautiful
to be worthy of being remembered.
wilted petals are a death sentence, so I pull
off the heads, yellowing leaves, anything to
make it photogenic again
I clear the blooms of insects and dirt as if I
am unearthing a tomb:
 here lies the beauty in imperfection, in
being a little different, or weird.
I brush it all away because no one wants to
see pictures of dirty flowers, and if no one
wants to see them, who will know that they
are beautiful?

Murky Waters

I feel like a home crumbling beneath my
own feet: my foundation has been cracked
from the beginning, built on too-soft ground,
I didn't stand a chance
the tiles are peeling in the kitchen from the
heat, pipes seconds from bursting
the water comes out black, and the only
thing the lights do consistently is flicker
the wires are too crossed to untangle, and we
are sinking into the swamp; murky waters
threatening to turn my lungs into fishbowls,
until I am merely a statue reclaimed by the
earth.
would it not be easier to start over? tear this
one down and rebuild, from the ground up?
Or at least move somewhere I do not feel
like I am drowning?
what I'm trying to say, is: maybe we should
not have built this house in the first place,
but it has always been my home
for all of their flaws, these walls have
always held me when I needed it most, so I
will return the favor. I will patch the holes in
the plaster, and tighten the leaky pipes

I will bail the swamp water out the door and
pull the foundation from the mud
when I am through, this house will finally
feel like home.

Untitled

please be careful with me
I have never been particularly careful with
myself, always the first to step into the
crosswalk, run across a busy street, daring
drivers to hit me as I went because if they're
going to hit anyone I would rather it be me

I am so quick to trust, heart in my hands,
ready to be yours for however long you want
it, despite how many times I have had to
stitch its bleeding wounds myself after they
have gone and left me for dead

I feel as if I am always walking on broken
legs, only ever making it worse, but they
said to walk it off and I believed them that
the problem would disappear like the
morning dew

I have shouldered my pain to carry it across
the river, but I am in the middle and it is
weighing me down, threatening to drag me

below the currents if I do not lighten my
load.
I did not realize that I could have set some
of this down.

Wondering: haunted

I always wondered if I would see him again
I thought that was what it meant to be
haunted
that I would see him around every corner,
perhaps he'd be in the background of all of
my polaroids,
behind me in every bathroom mirror
but I have not seen him since.
I still find myself glancing over my shoulder
on windy nights like this, wondering if I'll
catch a glimpse
maybe there is a perfectly rational
explanation for the man in the snow, maybe
I dreamt it all, maybe he was just a metaphor
for my depression that my young brain
thought I would understand
but I didn't, and when the panic died down, I
went back to slitting my wrists for the first
time
I wonder, was he trying to stop me?
maybe he was merely pushing me over the
edge

I still look for him, though, and maybe that's
what it means to be haunted

23

Persephone

while she is gone, the months growing
colder and the days growing shorter, that is
when I light the candles, swallow mouthfuls
of sweet pomegranate juice
I feel it slip down my esophagus, passing
my heart and lungs and taking root in my
belly. I will keep her warm here.
when the spring comes I will feel her
blossom again, life will begin anew as it
does every year
the cloud of winter lifts away and the sun
coaxes the crocuses from their beds, and she
will open her eyes, and together we will sit,
and listen to the birdsong
I will offer her honey made from
wildflowers and strawberries fresh from my
garden, and welcome her back to abundant
life

Higher Self

growing up I was always told to live my life
as close to God as possible, so is it any
wonder I am always chasing new highs?
they take me closer to the god that dwells
within me
I have glimpsed her
she is righteous fury on a cloudless day, wild
and haunted and free, a force with which to
be reckoned
I am working on rising to their level, like the
sea rising with the moon's pull
self care is turning into a spiritual
experience
the juice of a fresh peach dribbling down my
chin an act of worship
I have never noticed how perfectly my
fingers fit between each other until now, it is
as if interlacing them acts as prayer
I will turn this body back into the temple it
was meant to be
for how better to be close to God, than to
become her

soul searching below the poverty line

Is wandering through the dollar store, wondering if another "lavender" candle will finally bring it's promised serenity, if not, at least it smells nice and only cost $2

staring into the stars and dreaming of weightlessness, bouncing between nebulae, maybe new gravitational pulls will shift your spine back into place, chiropractic expenses be damned

hoarding the good fortunes from fortune cookies and treating them as gospel, papered across the walls as if writing your own prophecy, because "positivity attracts positivity"

if doing the backstroke through clouds with your brain were an Olympic sport, you would be a gold medalist, always tossing

what ifs at the ceiling but nothing ever
seems to stick for long enough

staring into your reflection in the windows
of the shops you cannot afford, pondering
who is gazing back: they look kinda like
you, they could be you, had fate dealt you a
different hand

Sonder

I step into the cool air of the night; push off
the wall and allow it to envelope me
completely, bathing myself in the feeling.
My eye is drawn to the window of a far-off
apartment building a mere breath before the
light flickers on-
not an uncommon occurrence-
and the sonder kicks in. I wonder what
mysterious being has flipped the switch,
what they are doing up so late

I wonder if they see my light and think a
similar thought, or what their kitchens smell
like at dinnertime, how their residents
navigate the halls late at night when the
lights are out

home is such a personal concept, but it can
be so elusive
I have been looking for mine for so long, but
it keeps slipping through my fingers like
sand
How will I know it when I find it?

Untitled

and overnight the winds may change
bringing with them new storms on the
horizon,
but for now,
reprieve,
a gentle sea breeze that carries tidings of rest
fasten the sails, batten the hatches, admire
the sea's docility; how pacific she can be
this is not a day for fighting the flurries of
fate
tomorrow we may take back up the
compass, continue fighting the tides
today, let us set the anchor for a time.

Untitled

Maybe black holes are just lonely
I mean
Does the chimney not also feel the burn of
smoke in her lungs
Perhaps the wildfire only spreads in an
attempt to smother herself
The stars only shine to guard their own eyes
from the light
What I mean to say is
Maybe they're all just trying their best

I am trying my best

Halfway

Are you an organized or messy person?
I'm messy
Everything about me is messy
My hair
My room
Even in my tidiest state I am a mess
From the fact that every item of clothing I
own is perpetually wrinkled,
To the green paint on my white ceiling
to the fact that I fall in love with like five
people that I do not know a day
akin many of my projects, I am started but
never quite finished
in my second year of university, I moved in
with a group of friends, where one of them
dubbed me "half fruit" for the halves I
would leave uneaten in the fridge
always in the middle of something and
forgetting what I was in the middle of
I am not really sure of anything; my
thoughts have a mind of their own and a
tendency to daydream

I have grown so tired from jumping down
the rabbit holes of my attention span, please,
just meet me halfway

Wildflower: Weed

I've been digging out the roots of what you
planted in me
seeds carelessly scattered in a fertile field
that you allowed to grow, hell, even watered
occasionally
but now you look at the flowers she has
borne and call her weed
you see her bright colours, and her tendency
to take over, and her medicinal properties,
and decide that weed is too much!
so what do you do? you spray weed with
poison and lies until she believes that she
will never be good enough to be considered
flower
to be considered beauty instead of pest
you say the only way weed will ever be
flower is if she grows solely where you
allow her, but that is not how growth works
you cannot control where, or how, or when it
happens
the next time you look at her and decide she
needs to shrink herself, just remember that
weed knows what soil is best for her roots
better than anyone, especially you.

Goddess Trine

maidens masquerading as mother and crone
but they still cannot heal the wounds of their
own
so on me it lands
now in my hands
is the fate of my family mine alone?
are their third eyes truly that tightly closed?

just another sexual assault poem

the first time it happened, I didn't realize
what she had done. I remembered the feeling
that burgeoned through my chest, though.
the feeling of fear, of discomfort in my own
skin.
I had believed that I was safe here.
it wasn't until the second time that I pieced it
together, cemented it in the third. they all
took so easily, ignoring all of my cues. I
used to think it's a good thing it happened to
me, and not some other girl, that I was
strong enough to handle it, that there's no
way this would break me. Boy was I wrong.
The pain merely needed time to fester.
until it rotted its way through my gut and
into my womb, and grew into new
distortions I am unlearning
additionally, running into one of the people
who assaulted you semi-regularly is enough
to make anyone begin to question their life
choices, but that is the problem with coming

home, it always puts me back between the
snake's ribs, as if they have been digesting
me all along
I am trying to learn that it was not my fault.
that there is nothing inherent in me that
evokes bloodthirst
but learning is always a process.

this is my suicide note.

I keep it on me like a cyanide pill: just in
case of emergency
if the pain, the stress of just being alive, ever
becomes too much, I know I will only have
to bite the bullet
I have already dug the grave, I might as well
lie in it
my body has always just been a corpse
waiting to decompose, to become one with
the earth in the most intimate way I can
imagine
I will be long gone by the time the poppies
bloom through my rib cage on to new
adventures, brighter pastures
and maybe the grass is always greener, but
maybe, the sky is bluer, too, maybe I can
feel the heat of the sun on my face and feel
grateful to be alive, or look at a length of
rope without seeing a noose
maybe, I will learn to look forward to
tomorrow
I could not find a way to make this skin feel
like home, so I will merely try again.

I am content watching you be happy

I am content watching you be happy
but I still wonder how your lips would feel
pressed against mine
I want to feel the rumble of your laugh
against my back as we play video games on
the couch
how your arms feel gently encasing mine,
thumbs connecting constellations in my
freckles while I gaze into the depth of your
eyes
I want to hold you so close, show you how
dear you are to me
get to know the weight of your palm in my
own, how our fingers entwine with each
other
but then I see you with them, and I see that
you have that already
so I am content with seeing you happy

Untitled

I see adventure in your eyes
blue skies over the open road of your smile
you are the breeze through my open window
fingers as they wave along to the radio
the open arms of my impala after a long day
at work, the freedom we share in those
intimate first moments when the possibilities
are endless and the gas tank is full
I want to drive to where the streetlights can't
reach us just so I can see the moonlight on
your skin, so I can study the reflections of
the stars in your eyes, match constellations
to the freckles that dot your body

Untitled

I go on a long and arduous journey through
the underworld to find medusa
I tell her that she is the most beautiful
woman in the world to me
we kiss
partway through I open my eyes, my lips
slowly turning to stone
this having been my plan all along

fountain of youth

the clouds are gone, the sky is blue
is this the fount' of eternal youth?
it's hot as hades,
no moisture dusts the air
but we have lakes and streams and ponds
and they hold their fair share
so if the heat you cannot handle do not feel
despair
simply find a shady pond and tumble
headfirst into there

Zug Zwang

I keep telling myself not to idealize you, to
daydream our perfect life so much I forget to
pay attention
that that's what I did wrong last time

but then I think of my daydreams about our
life together and I know I don't need to
the life I picture with you is simple,
something I've always known

you are my checkmate

Icarus

as I lay here
gazing at the vast blue expanse above my
head
I envy the man with wings of wax
at least he was able to kiss the sun,
thank her for her warmth
before he fell

The life cycle of seasonal depression
and suddenly, the darkness of winter lifts, if
only for a moment, but it is enough to hope,
to recall the memory of warmth
so you pick yourself up, as if spring Herself
has touched your soul, and soak in the calm
blue sky, the sunlight on your cheeks, with
the remembrance that you will be warm
again

Untitled

Laughter blooms against our ceiling
We have a magnolia that blooms out front in
the spring, but it is nothing like our
Laughter: it's petals soft and pure
we are all impurities and sharp edges we are
trying to sand
Laughter like off-brand, day old champagne
The spark is still there, it merely needs
coaxing, but it will heat you up nicely

Untitled

hold me until you can hold me no longer
let me watch the seasons pass from your
embrace
in the summer be my shade, in the winter
my sunshine
forever yours I'll remain, as long as you'll be
mine